Tale of a Tadpole

Written by Karen Wallace

Series Editor Deborah Lock
US Senior Editor Shannon Beatty
Project Editors Caroline Bingham, Caryn Jenner, Penny Smith
Editors Regina Kahney, Arpita Nath, Anneka Wahlhaus
Art Editor Jyotsna Julka, Michelle Baxter
Senior Art Editor Ann Cannings
Producer Christine Ni
Senior Producer, Pre-production Francesca Wardell
Picture Researcher Sakshi Saluja
Jacket Designer Hoa Luc
DTP Designers Nand Kishor Acharya,
Vijay Kandwal, Nityanand Kumar, Anita Yadav
Managing Editor Soma B. Chowdhury
Managing Art Editor Ahlawat Gunjan
Art Directors Rachel Foster, Martin Wilson
Editorial Consultant Theresa Greenaway

Reading Consultant
Linda Gambrell, Ph.D.

First American Edition, 1998
Other editions, 2009, 2010
This edition, 2015
Published in the United States by DK Publishing
1450 Broadway, New York, New York 10018

Copyright © 1998, 2015 Dorling Kindersley Limited
A Penguin Random House Company
21 22 10 9 8
008—271724—Oct/15

A catalog record for this book is available
from the Library of Congress.

ISBN: 978-1-4654-3508-8 (Paperback)
ISBN: 978-1-4654-3509-5 (Hardcover)

DK books are available at special discounts when purchased in bulk for sales promotions,
premiums, fund-raising, or educational use. For details, contact: DK Publishing Special Markets,
1450 Broadway, New York, New York 10018
SpecialSales@dk.com

Printed in China

The publisher would like to thank the following for their kind permission to reproduce their photographs:
(Key: a=above, b=below/bottom, c=center, l=left, r=right, t=top)
Photographers: Paul Bricknell, Jane Burton, Geoff Dann, Mike Dunning, Neil Fletcher, Frank Greenaway and Kim Taylor.
4-5 Dreamstime.com: Chudtsankov. **5 Alamy Images:** David Cook / blueshiftstudios (r). **6-7 Dreamstime.com:**
Chudtsankov. **6 Alamy Images:** David Cook / blueshiftstudios (cl). **Dorling Kindersley:** Jerry Young (b). **7 Corbis:** David A.
Northcott (cl); DLILLC (br). **18 Dreamstime.com:** Anna Bakulina (t). **iStockphoto.com:** Gannet77 (ca).
18-19 Dreamstime.com: Chudtsankov. **19 Dorling Kindersley:** Twan Leenders (c). **30-31 Dreamstime.com:**
Chudtsankov. **30 Dreamstime.com:** Andreykuzmin (ca); Danny Smythe (tl). **38-39 Dreamstime.com:** Chudtsankov.
Getty Images: James Balog (Frog). **42-43 Dreamstime.com:** Chudtsankov. **42 Alamy Images:** David Cook /
blueshiftstudios (cl). **Dreamstime.com:** Isselee (cr). **44 Dreamstime.com:** Mgkuijpers (br).
Science Photo Library: Claude Nuridsany & Marie Perennou (bl).
Jacket images: Front: Getty Images: parema / E+ t.
All other images © Dorling Kindersley
For further information see: www.dkimages.com

A WORLD OF IDEAS:
SEE ALL THERE IS TO KNOW

Contents

A Tadpole is a Baby Frog

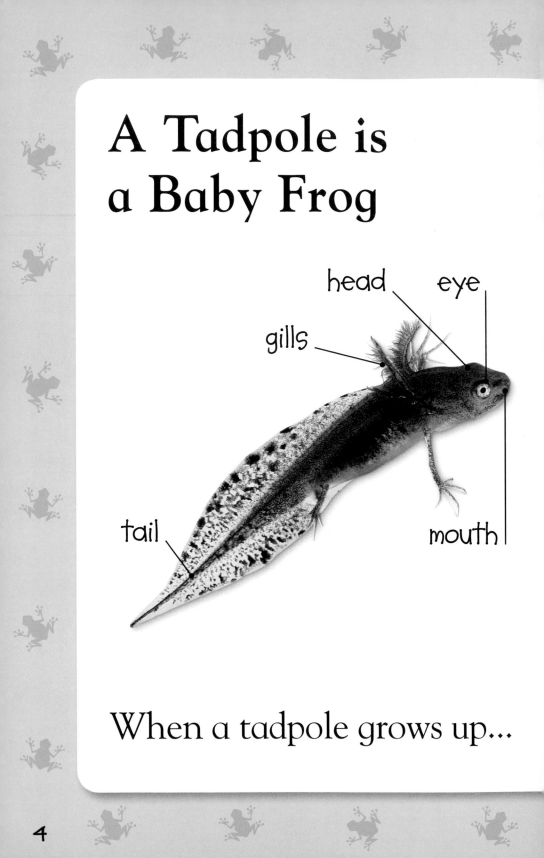

head

eye

gills

tail

mouth

When a tadpole grows up...

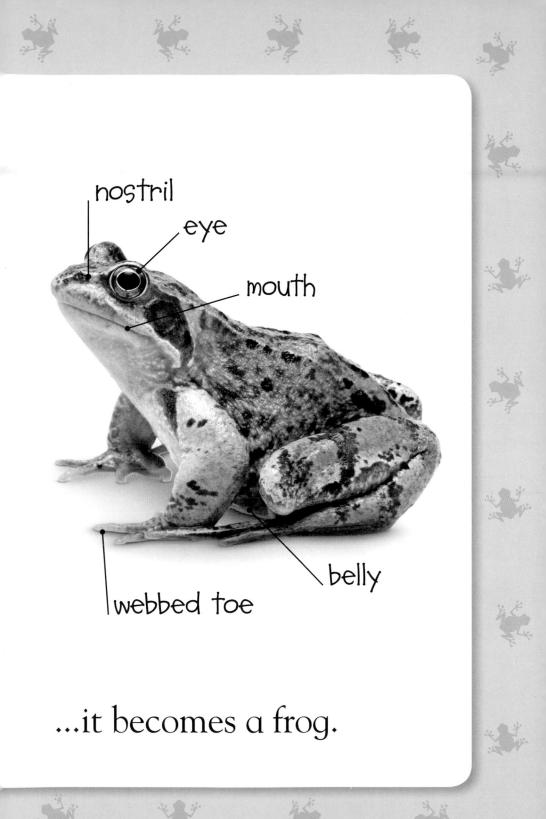

nostril

eye

mouth

belly

webbed toe

...it becomes a frog.

Frog Gallery

There are more than 4,000 kinds of frogs. They are different shapes, sizes, and colors.

Common frogs

live near ponds and in tall grass.

Green ornate horned frogs

use their big mouths to eat a lot of food.

Malayan leaf frogs

look like leaves.
This helps them
to hide on the
forest floor and
hunt for food.

Mantellas

are found in many
different colors.

Red-eyed
tree frogs

scare enemies
with their big,
red eyes.

The tale of a tadpole
begins in a pond.
Mother frog lays her eggs
next to a lily pad.

Each tiny egg is wrapped
in clear jelly.

Inside the jelly,
the eggs grow into tadpoles.
They wriggle like worms.

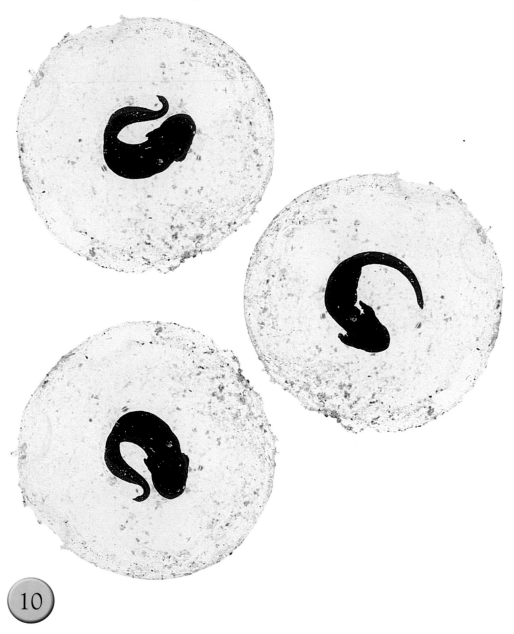

They push through the jelly
and swim in the water.

They breathe through gills,
just like fish.

Many other animals
live in the pond.

There are shiny goldfish and
sticklebacks and
great diving beetles.

They chase the young tadpoles.

A stickleback feels hungry.
He opens his mouth wide.

The little gray tadpoles
wriggle their tails…

…and swim away
through the water.

A great diving beetle
feels hungry too.

His hairy back legs
beat through the water.

The tadpoles escape
and hide in the weeds.

Frog Facts

A mother frog can lay as many as 4,000 eggs at once.

The egg jelly has food inside for the growing tadpoles.

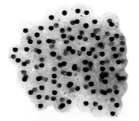

A group of frog eggs is called frog spawn.

Summer is the best time to spot new adult frogs.

Frogs call to one another by croaking.

A frog's skin is wet and slippery.

Most tadpoles are eaten by other animals before they grow into frogs.

Soon a tadpole
grows legs
with tiny webbed toes.

Webbed toes are like flippers.
They help the small tadpole
push through the water.

He grows arms
with long skinny fingers.

He nibbles on plants and
gobbles green pondweed.

Half tadpole, half frog,
he rests in the sunshine.

His tail is shrinking.

It gets smaller and smaller.

The new little frog
sits on a lily pad.

His legs are strong now.
He can breathe
through his nostrils.
His skin is dotted
with tiny gold spots.

Frogs must keep their skin slimy.
He hops back in the pond
and swims for a while.
Then he climbs onto a log.

Another frog climbs up
and sits down beside him.

Build a Frog Home

You will need:

 trowel    watering can

clay pot   gravel

soil   saucer

damp leaves

1   Use a trowel to dig a hole in a damp place. Half-fill a clay pot with soil and damp leaves. Put it on its side in the hole.

2 Use a watering can to wet the area. This will hold the pot in place.

3 Put gravel and water in a saucer. Place it next to the pot so the frog can splash around!

Now full-grown,
he dives through the water.

He's not afraid of the stickleback.
He swims past the beetle.

In the pond,
he watches and waits.
What does he see
with his round beady eyes?

A fly lands
above him.
He creeps
closer and closer.

But a big frog jumps up.
It snatches the fly
with its long, sticky tongue.

The frog
misses his meal.
Next time
he'll be faster!

Hop Like a Frog

Frogs have long back legs that help them to hop high and far.

Can you hop like a frog?

The golden-skinned frog
chases a dragonfly.
It lands on a lily pad.
Under the lily pad are
hundreds of frogs' eggs.

Inside each egg,
a tadpole is growing.
Each tadpole will grow
into a new frog.

From Tadpole to Frog

The tadpole hatches out of the egg.

It has a tail and lives in water.

The tadpole has become a frog.

The tadpole grows feet and teeth.

Tadpole Quiz

 1 What is wrapped around the tiny frog eggs?

 2 What do tadpoles breathe through?

 3 Which has a tail —a tadpole or a frog?

 4 What is a group of frog eggs called?

 5 How do frogs call to one another?

Answers on page 45.

Glossary

gills openings in a tadpole's body used to breathe under water

jelly covering that protects frog eggs

nostrils two openings on a frog's face used to breathe

tail back end of the tadpole's body

tongue long, sticky muscle in a frog's mouth used to catch food

webbed toe skin between toes that helps tadpoles to swim

Index

Answers to the Tadpole Quiz:

1. Clear jelly; **2.** Gills; **3.** Tadpole;
4. Frog spawn; **5.** By croaking.

Guide for Parents

DK Readers is a four-level interactive reading adventure series for children, developing the habit of reading widely for both pleasure and information. These books have an exciting main narrative interspersed with a range of reading genres to suit your child's reading ability, as required by the Common Core State Standards. Each book is designed to develop your child's reading skills, fluency, grammar awareness, and comprehension in order to build confidence and engagement when reading.

Ready for a *Beginning to Read* book

YOUR CHILD SHOULD

- be familiar with using beginning letter sounds and context clues to figure out unfamiliar words.
- be aware of the need for a slight pause at commas and a longer one at periods.
- alter his/her expression for questions and exclamations.

A VALUABLE AND SHARED READING EXPERIENCE

For many children, reading requires much effort, but adult participation can make this both fun and easier. So here are a few tips on how to use this book with your child.

TIP 1 Check out the contents together before your child begins:

- read the text about the book on the back cover.
- flip through the book and and stop to chat about the contents page together to heighten your child's interest and expectation.
- make use of unfamiliar or difficult words on the page in a brief discussion.
- chat about the nonfiction reading features used in the book, such as headings, captions, recipes, lists, or charts.

TIP 2 Support your child as he/she reads the story pages:

- give the book to your child to read and turn the pages.
- where necessary, encourage your child to break a word into syllables, sound out each one, and then flow the syllables together. Ask him/her to reread the sentence to check the meaning.
- when there's a question mark or an exclamation mark, encourage your child to vary his/her voice as he/she reads the sentence. Demonstrate how to do this if it is helpful.

TIP 3 Chat at the end of each page:

- the factual pages tend to be more difficult than the story pages, and are designed to be shared with your child.
- ask questions about the text and the meaning of the words used. These help to develop comprehension skills and awareness of the language used.

A FEW ADDITIONAL TIPS

- Always encourage your child to try reading difficult words by themselves. Praise any self-corrections, for example, "I like the way you sounded out that word and then changed the way you said it, to make sense."
- Try to read together everyday. Reading little and often is best. These books are divided into manageable chapters for one reading session. However, after 10 minutes, only keep going if your child wants to read on.
- Read other books of different types to your child just for enjoyment and information.

Series consultant, **Dr. Linda Gambrell**, Distinguished Professor of Education at Clemson University, has served as President of the National Reading Conference, the College Reading Association, and the International Reading Association. She is also reading consultant for the **DK Adventures**.

Have you read these other great books from DK?

BEGINNING TO READ ①

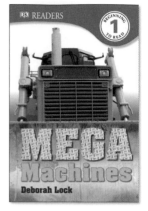

Splash! A young dolphin explores the ocean, diving and leaping.

Find out what happens on a farm through the seasons.

Hard hats on! Watch the busy machines build a new school.

BEGINNING TO READ ALONE ②

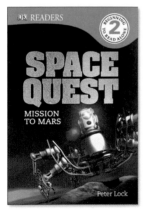

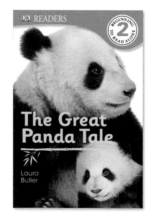

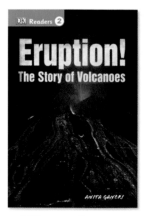

Embark on a mission to explore the solar system. First stop—Mars.

Join Louise at the zoo, preparing to welcome a new panda baby.

What spits out fire and ash or explodes with a bang? Volcanoes!